I0437990

The Girl

and the

Big Brown Horse

Sue M. Healy

authorHOUSE®

AuthorHouse™
1663 Liberty Drive, Suite 200
Bloomington, IN 47403
www.authorhouse.com
Phone: 1-800-839-8640

© 2009 Sue M. Healy. All rights reserved.

No part of this book may be reproduced, stored in a retrieval system, or transmitted by any means without the written permission of the author.

First published by AuthorHouse 6/9/2009

ISBN: 978-1-4389-4790-7 (sc)

Library of Congress Control Number: 2009900769

Printed in the United States of America
Bloomington, Indiana

This book is printed on acid-free paper.

DEDICATION

I dedicate this book to Syndraff (Syn), who gave his entire existence to my happiness and who helped me to see the world through his eyes and his spirit. Syn possessed such great qualities - kindness, sensibility, nobility, and heart. I shall never forget our days together for the rest of my life. Not a single day passes that I do not think of Syn and remember with great fondness our many wonderful adventures.

Over the thirty years of our intense companionship, we traveled thousands of miles together; through lush open green landscapes rich with wildflowers and butterflies in early spring; to hot and dusty roads and trails in the summer heat; on into the cool and glorious vibrant Michigan Autumn colors as we galloped up grassy hills rustling up deer and quail;

and finally into the bitter-cold icy winter fields dressed for sub-freezing temperatures. Season after season, year upon year, we rode together in all weather. We never missed a day of riding in our younger years and he always carried me safely through all terrains and under all conditions.

My family never worried about me when I rode Syn cross country alone because he was so sure-footed and careful with me. On one occasion in my younger years, when I was attempting to urge Syn through a particularly gnarly path covered in deep winter snow, he was refusing to move forward in the trail. I tried to push him on and I was becoming rather annoyed with him until I noticed a partially obscured strand of barbed-wire fencing below the snow-bank's surface. At a minimum, this fencing would have tripped us causing a treacherous fall and possible injury to both of us. It was then that I put my full trust in him and we became inseparable. He also began to put his complete trust in me after several years of riding and his mind was like second nature to me, never hesitating, never faltering, and never questioning my guidance and direction. We truly rode as one; one spirit with inseparable and kindred heart and soul.

Now that Syn is gone from my life and as I age, I reminisce more and I am becoming more soft-hearted and sensitive. I now realize that Syn was "the one great horse" that each of us gets in this lifetime we are given.

Through my acquaintances, I have come to understand that in any individual's lifetime, we can never have more than one great dog or one great horse. All future dogs and horses are forever measured against this special one; rather like the gold standard... I have had many other horses come into my life since Syn's death, but none have remotely approached his capabilities nor have any inched their way into the soft spots of my heart and soul. Almost as if some portion of my spirit has left this earth to reside in another dimension with him....

My wish for every horse-lover everywhere in the world is that you too will find that one "great" horse to fulfill your dreams. I hope that you too will be blessed with echoing hoofbeats in your heart, and you also will be left a better person for that special horse having shared their life with you.....

ACKNOWLEDGMENT ...

This book is written for all of the women around the world who know and share my deepest love for horses; and there are many. I have had the opportunity to know and to develop deep friendships with so many wonderful horse-loving people over my lifetime.

I want to give special thanks and appreciation to my oldest son, Cyrus, who has given me continual encouragement to write my story and publish this book. During the past two very difficult years, he has been a pillar in my life; a rock to cling to and remind me of what is important in life. His wisdom and support have given me the strength and courage to complete this project despite the difficult, stressful, almost insurmountable challenges in my life.

And I need to give a special thanks to my husband, who, although he has never shared my deep love for horses, has tolerated my love for them and has worked to provide me with a beautiful environment and ample provisions for my horse-passion.

And, finally, I would like to thank both my mother and my father. My mother, Leona Holodnick, who helped persuade my father that I should have my very first horse. She knew me so well and loved me so much, that she made certain my dream of owning a horse became a reality. And my father, John Holodnick, who helped me construct the little horse barn on our farm. While he initially challenged the entire horse investment, he later admitted (shortly before he passed away), that "allowing me to have a horse was the best thing he ever did for me..."

I also want to thank all of the horses and ponies who have come into my life since Syn moved on to Heaven's greener pastures. They have tried to fill the void and hollowness that Syn has left in my heart and in my life. And, while none will ever live up to the same level of expectation, I have had the comfort and joy of sharing my life with several wonderful, giving, and very honest ponies and horses since that time; Merrywill's Crystal Moon (Moon Mare), Postmaster General (Leo), Napoleon (Pony Man), Sparky (Sparkman), and of course Khemosabi Sun (Sabi). I love them all and continue to enjoy their presence in my life.

Thanks to all of you.....

Forward

"Some horses come into our life and quickly leave.
Others stay awhile; make hoofprints in our hearts,
and we are never the same again....."
(Author Unknown)

The Girl

and the

Big Brown Horse

The little girl loved horses from the very first moment that she could remember. It was as if something from the depths of her soul called her mysteriously toward the wondrous hooved creatures and the bond that a girl and a horse can share.

From her earliest days as a child, she was fascinated by and drawn to the beauty and magnificence of horses. As a toddler, she loved to dress up in western outfits and pretend to be a cowgirl with a hundred fantastic cowponies and wild mustangs to choose from.

When the little girl was a little bit older, she attended school, but she often found it difficult to stay focused on the subjects the teachers presented. It seemed as if the class dawdled on simple topics, allowing the young girl's mind to wander. She would sketch her favorite subject with her lead pencil on lined school paper, creating drawings of beautiful horses and elegant ponies with flowing manes and tails in fantastic poses. Each picture was an effort to improve upon the one that was created the day before.

When she got home, she would tape the pictures to her bedroom wall and then lie on her bed, staring at them and dreaming of the day when she would have a beautiful horse of her own. The dream would always end sadly, though, for she would realize that her parents could not afford to buy her a horse.

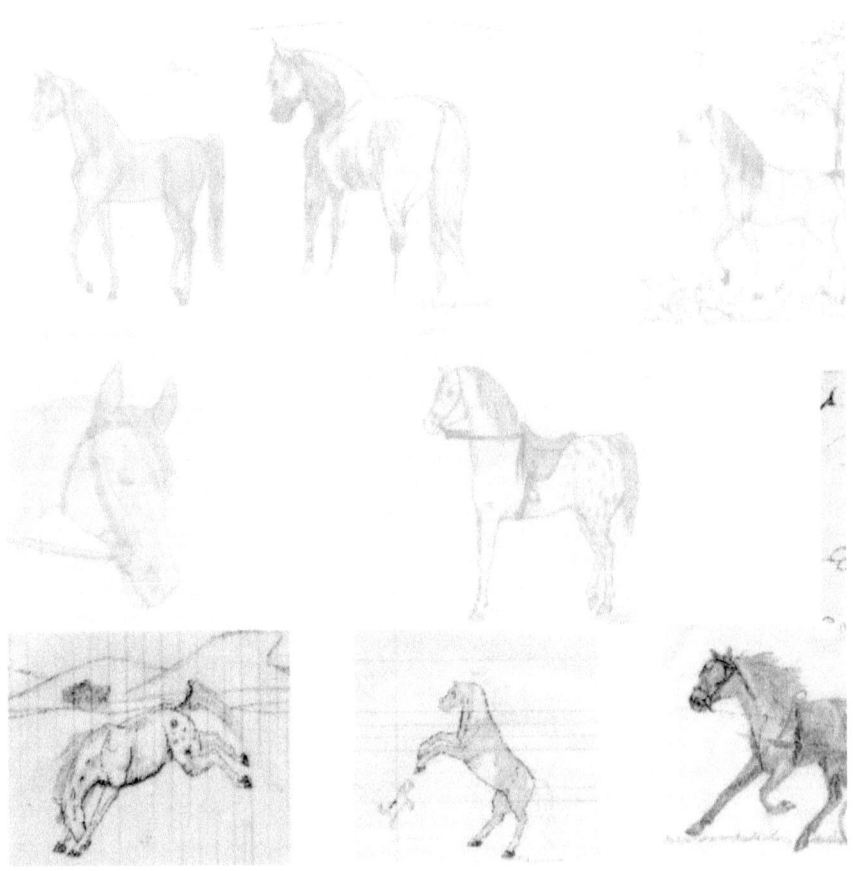

People with similar interests tend to be drawn together, and the young girl soon became best friends with another student who owned two beautiful chestnut-colored Welsh Mountain ponies.

Sometimes the young girl would accompany her friend home on the school bus. The two young girls would ride the plump, gentle ponies for hours; talking, laughing, and enjoying their long rides through the woods and hills and beaches, with the sun shining warmly on their backs and the lake wind blowing in their faces.

After riding, she would lovingly brush the pony's thick fur and untangle the long silky tail of the pony she had ridden. Then as a special treat for the pony, she shucked the hard golden kernels from a cob of corn and, cupping the kernels into her hands, offered them to the pony to eat. She loved the feel of the pony's soft warm nose against the callused palms of her young hands.

It was always great fun, but upon returning home, she again dreamed of having her very own horse with which she could build a strong, permanent bond.

Her dream became more deeply embedded in her mind, and she was saddened to think how far off that day might still be.

With two working parents and six children in the family, she had many responsibilities at home, including much of the housecleaning, cooking, and baby-sitting.

But, day after day, she had only one dream in her mind: to have a horse of her very own.

Whenever she was not in school and not needed for work at home, she began taking on work outside of the home; any jobs that she could find, doing whatever she could to earn money to make her dream come true.

During the summer, she worked for neighboring farmers baling hay and straw. The work was very strenuous for the young girl, but she worked side by side with her three older brothers stacking the heavy hay bales onto the farm wagons or into the hot, dusty haylofts in the farmer's barns.

During the evenings she performed baby-sitting duties for numerous local families for fifty cents an hour, and on Saturdays she did housecleaning for some of the neighboring elders. If transportation could not be provided, she walked or rode her bicycle to the jobs.

One year, she bought some white mice and borrowed a glass fish tank from an older brother to house them in. For nearly two years she raised litters of white mice and sold dozens of baby white mice for fifty cents each to other schoolchildren for pets or science fair projects.

The money accumulated slowly, but every cent that could be saved was placed in an old wooden cigar box labeled "Horse Money," which she kept hidden under her bed.

And while other girls her age were buying makeup, pretty dresses, and tickets to the local dances, she was working every opportunity she had and saving all of her earnings to make her dream come true.

Then one day the young girl learned of an Arabian horse farm that was a two-hour drive from the family's home. She had often cut pictures of this stunning breed of horses from newspapers and magazines for her horse scrapbook. Although she knew that she could not afford a purebred Arabian, she was captivated with the thought of seeing a real live Arabian horse.

She wrote a letter to the owner of the farm, and in her letter she told the woman how she had earned nearly three hundred dollars and how desperately she wanted a horse of her own. She pleaded in her letter for the woman to consider making a deal on any horse that she owned.

Several months passed, and the young girl had nearly given up hope. Then one day the young girl was surprised to receive a response from the horse farm in the mail. The farm owner had written her a long letter explaining that because of the exceptional bloodlines, their horses sold for many thousands of dollars.

The girl's heart sank and tears welled in her eyes as she read on about all of the spectacular attributes and qualities of their beautiful well-bred Arabian horses.

However, at the close of the letter, the owner stated that she had one older part-Arabian broodmare that was due to foal in about six months.

If the baby horse was a filly, it had already been sold to another family. But if the baby horse was a colt, she would consider selling him to the young girl for the three hundred dollars she had saved.

The young girl was ecstatic, and she begged her parents incessantly to allow her to purchase the horse; they finally, reluctantly, consented.

The young girl mailed a thank-you note and a deposit on the baby horse, which she prayed each night would be a colt. It was the longest six months of the young girl's life, waiting for the word to come.

Then, one bitter-cold early February morning, she received a telephone call. The mare had given birth to a large bay colt, which they had nicknamed "Igloo" since he had been born on the day of the coldest recorded temperature in the history of the state of Michigan.

The young girl begged her parents to take her that very weekend to see the baby horse.

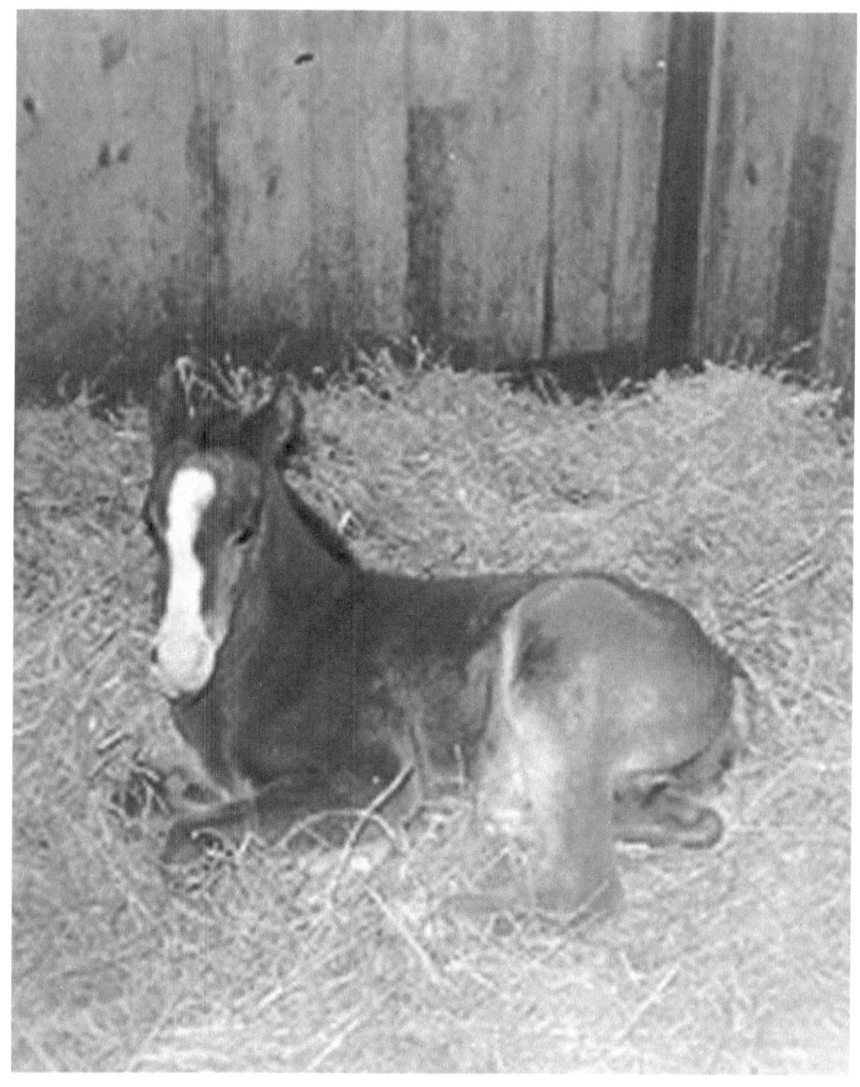

As the stall door slid open, the young girl got her first look at him. From the first time she gazed upon him she knew that he was unbelievably special.

She stood in awe, for at only three days of age, the colt stood tall and proud on strong, straight legs. His delicate pointed ears were tipped inward; his eyes were large, dark, and intelligent. His tiny nose was covered with long whiskers that were frosted from the sub-zero temperatures. His coat, although long for the cold season, was a rich dark brown. He had four white socks and a generous white blaze spilling wildly down his forehead and covering his nose.

With confidence the baby colt immediately walked up to the young girl and placed his nose inquisitively against her arm, and then he lifted his tiny head, looked into her eyes, and breathed his warm breath into her face.

For the young girl, it was love at first sight!!!!

Who will ever know for certain if this colt really *was* born to be special, or if it was that the young girl's love and unending faith in his ability would *make* him special; but whatever the reason, he was to live up to her every expectation . . .

When the colt was three months old, he was delivered to the young girl's home where the girl's father had helped her build a stall and mend the little barn that was on the family's little farm.

When the horse trailer arrived and the baby horse backed out of it, he whinnied boldly.

The young girl put her arms around his tiny neck in a warm and welcoming hug.

The young girl pressed her lips against his tiny ear and whispered that she would love him and take care of him forever.

Then the young girl led him to the small box stall upon which she had inscribed his name, and he immediately made himself at home . . .

The young girl gave the baby horse the registered name of Syndraff but nicknamed him "Syn."

Every spare moment of the girl's life was spent lovingly attending to the baby horse. Since he was too young to ride, she spent hours brushing his coat, combing his dark, fluffy baby mane and tail, and handling each hoof.

Every time she went to the barn, she would gently place his soft halter onto his head and lead him around the farm or down the country road. He soon walked beside her without any rope between them, connected only by the strength of their love and his desire to please the young girl.

The young girl continued to work at whatever jobs she could find to earn money, which she used to buy hay, grain, and the tack and equipment that was needed as he continued to steadily outgrow his halters and blankets.

At mealtimes, as a treat for the young horse, the young girl would carefully cut the family's fruits and vegetables, saving the apple peelings or carrot tops. He was particularly fond of watermelon rinds, and after the family's summer meals, the young girl would gather them up and take them to him. He delighted in making a foamy, slobbery mess of eating the watery rinds!!!

Sometimes on hot summer days, the girl would take her reading books out to the small fenced-in field behind their house and sit on the ground in the middle of the young horse's paddock to read. The young horse's curiosity was too great to ignore the situation, for he would immediately circle the girl several times and then carefully lower his large frame to the ground to lie down beside her and she would read to him, enjoying the closeness of their friendship.

When the young horse was nearly two years old, the young girl placed a long rope on his halter and trained him to lunge by gently encouraging him to run large circles around her. He was a fast and willing learner and soon was performing all gaits by responding to her voice commands.

One day when the young horse had grown strong enough to support a rider, the young girl lead him alongside of a stack of straw bales. Quietly and gently, she slid onto his back. She braced herself for whatever wild moves he might offer, but he merely turned his neck around and looked at her as if to say, "What took you so long?" It was as if he had known this day was inevitable and was overjoyed at the closeness between them. The young girl was ecstatic with joy that he accepted her weight upon his back without any resistance or worry.

The young girl could not afford to buy a saddle, so she rode him bareback. He was a gallant steed, boldly taking on any obstacle or terrain that his young rider asked of him. No horse of finer breeding could have shown more heart. He willingly responded to the young girl's voice commands as they galloped through open fields, wooded trails, stony country roads, rivers, lakes, and sandy dunes.

Sometimes the young girl borrowed a saddle and loaded him up with all the things needed for a camping trip. During summer vacation, the young girl and her sister, who now also had a pony, would ride to their grandmother's woods along the river and spend several days camping out among the trees and wild berry bushes.

They would lay open their bedrolls under the starry night sky and build a campfire to cook their food. With the horses tied to nearby trees, they would pretend they were living on their own in the middle of a wild and savage land.

Sometimes neighbors of the young girl took her and the young horse to local horse shows to compete. The judges could not help but notice this flashy young horse with the velvety dappled-brown coat. With his confident manner, he always pranced elegantly into the show ring; neck proudly arched, mane and tail flowing, his huge floating stride. He loved to hear the spectators clap and cheer, and he never failed to put on his showiest personality in the show ring, which consistently rewarded them with ribbons and trophies at local horse events.

Eventually the young girl was able to purchase a saddle and began riding him western, to which he eagerly and quickly adapted.

When the young girl graduated from high school, she attended a large state university, but it was overwhelming for the shy country girl. She enrolled in the pre-veterinary program, which was not then eagerly accepting women into this curriculum. It was difficult for her, and after several terms her scholarship money was exhausted. She had to make a choice between borrowing many thousands of dollars or doing something else.

Her heart longed for the comfort of her best friend, whom she had left behind at her parent's farm, and she missed their daily rides in the country. So she decided to take schooling in something that she really had her deepest love for . . . riding.

She applied for an internship at an out-of-state equestrian riding academy. The young woman was accepted and was allowed to take her young horse with her.

There she worked long days as a stable hand in the horse barns, mucking out stalls, grooming and feeding horses, and tacking up the school's lesson horses. The hard work was in exchange for living quarters and daily riding lessons by renowned equestrian instructors.

The young horse also worked hard at the academy, and together they learned the fine art of English riding.

Syn was a very flashy young horse and surprised the riding instructors with his ability to jump the same tall fences as the giant thoroughbred school horses. When the young woman rode him, he exhibited such animation and character that no one could ignore him when he entered the ring!

His tail would arch high over his back, and his flashy, animated stride would cause onlookers to turn their heads and watch him. He had a presence about him; something almost *magical* to watch.

Perhaps he *was* exceptionally gifted, or perhaps it was the mere *want* in him to do his absolute best for the young woman on his back . . .

Because he was so gentle and friendly with the many students who came daily to the school for riding lessons, he quickly became a favorite at the farm, and children regularly brought treats for him each time they came to the stable for riding lessons. He would gingerly accept the treats from the often-timid riders so as not to frighten them. He was loved by all of the children who came to the riding school.

The young woman and the horse worked hard together every day in grueling winter temperatures and in the hot summer sun; riding in outdoor rings and indoor arenas as the solemn instructors snapped verbal commands.

On afternoons when the young woman did not have to work in the stables, she would saddle the young horse and hand-gallop across the hundreds of acres of maple woods that were part of the riding school. The woods were filled with many miles of trails spotted with fallen trees, wooden fences, and stone walls, which they playfully hopped over.

She talked to the horse as if he were a person, and somehow just talking aloud to him made her feel better. It was a beautiful farm and a glorious place to be for both of them!!

After completing her equestrian training at the riding school, the young woman accepted a position at a private hunt stable in her home state, where she lived with a middle-aged couple. The couple offered her a place in their home, giving her the same privileges as a daughter, and they also allowed her to bring her horse to their farm.

Twice a week the local hunt club sponsored foxhunting events. After tacking up the boarder's horses, the stable owner allowed her to ready her wonderful young horse. The young woman and her horse were allowed to ride the hunt course at the rear of the hunt pack as guests since they were not official members.

It was a wonderful time for both of them, meeting new friends and building confidence in their newly learned riding skills. The hunt course varied over many miles of rugged terrain with wooden, stone, and natural jumps of all sizes and shapes.

The hunts lasted nearly all day, and the thrill of galloping headlong over fields and bounding over high fences was thrilling to both of them.

The young horse proved to be an excellent cross-country jumper and quickly earned the respect of his fellow huntsmen.

After her job ended there, the young woman and the horse moved back to her home area, where the young woman began working at a local factory. She met a young man at her workplace, and they later married. Although he did not share her strong love for horses, he accepted them and encouraged them because he knew how much they meant to his wife.

When they settled into their first little farmhouse, the horse accompanied them, and he quickly adjusted to their new life.

Some years passed, and the young woman had two sons. When they were infants, she would lift them unto the horse's back and lead the giggling boys around the barnyard. As small children, both boys learned to ride with confidence on the horse.

When the sons were riding, the horse would walk slowly and sedately around the barnyard, being extremely careful not to make any sudden movements that might unseat or alarm them while the reins slapped loosely at his neck.

When the boys dismounted and the woman climbed into the saddle, Syn's ears would perk up and he would stomp his feet and give a playful but gentle rocking-horse buck. The woman would have to take a tight rein to control his explosive energy. He loved to exhibit his playfulness and show off for her!

Other horses then became a part of the family's riding stock, but the big bay horse was always the family favorite and the leader of the pack.

He was the strongest and the bravest of the farm animals and enjoyed the status of being the dominant horse when they were turned out to pasture together. He would chase and frolic with the younger horses on the farm, eventually gaining the lead position, where he would run with the pack of horses. He was a magnificent animal to watch in action!!

Sue M. Healy

The woman was now reaching middle age, and the old horse was more than twenty-five years old. Her family returned to the country and settled into a beautiful farmhouse where the old horse had the run of the farm.

The horse was beginning to show his age a bit, but the middle-aged woman still took him out for a ride across the open countryside every opportunity she had in her busy schedule.

The woman now had two growing sons and a very high-stress management job filled with many impromptu business trips around the world. But whenever she had a bad day at work, she would saddle up the old horse and together they would slowly canter across the fields while she spilled all of her troubles upon his caring ears.

With his faithful, careful manners and attentive way of listening to her every word, he had a way of erasing all of the problems of her day. And she would tell him that after all these years; he was still her best friend.

The family's other horses were beginning to treat the old horse roughly by chasing him from the feed. He began to lose weight and look thin. This made the woman very sad, so the family constructed a special fence for him where he could be by himself and not have to fight for food. He could now walk right up to their back yard, observing the activities of the family.

The old horse was happy again. Every day the woman talked to the old horse, reminding him how much she loved him and what a good friend he was.

Whenever the woman appeared at the back door, the old horse would whinny to her and she would always call out his name and walk to him to stroke his forehead. She would stand with him for a few minutes and "chat" or feed him a treat from her hand. Then she would hug his thick, strong neck, and he would murmur a low soft response to her.

How comforting it still was to feel the warmth of his breath upon her hand, to feel the strength of him flowing through her in their hug, and to smell the sweetness of his neck against her face.

The years continued to pass, and the two friends aged together.

And then the day came that the middle-aged woman had been dreading for a very long time. The very old horse, who was now nearly thirty, began to look sickly and started losing a lot of weight.

The woman called veterinarians to the farm, specialists from around the area; but no one could offer help. The woman bought him special feeds and the family warmed it and fed him more often, but it did not help.

The old horse continued to lose weight.

And then he began coughing excessively for long periods of time every time he had eaten.

The woman made up a special place in the barn so that he could be warm and dry, but the very old horse grew more and more weary . . .

And then one cold October morning, he stopped eating completely.

The woman tried all of his favorite foods to get him to eat or drink, but he would not make any effort to eat what she presented to him.

After he had not had anything to eat or drink for three days, the woman again fetched some warm water, making one last attempt to encourage him to consume something, but the old horse refused to drink. The woman hugged his thin, emaciated neck and whispered a promise in his ear that he would suffer no more.

A veterinarian was again summoned to the farm, but this time to humanely end the life of her long-time friend so that he would endure pain and suffering no longer. The woman could not bear to allow her friend the slow, agonizing death that starvation brings.

The woman led the old horse slowly from his barn stall. His walk was labored and difficult. Lifting each foot was an almost impossible task, and he moaned in protest. But finally they stood together outside in the unseasonably cold autumn air.

The wind was brutal, and the old horse could barely stand on his own, so the woman placed an arm on his neck to steady his weak and tired body.

The last hug was a long and difficult one for the woman. How could she let this lifelong friend go?

This friend, who had shared her most intimate secrets and personal difficulties.

This friend, who had seen her through every inner conflict, personal struggle, career hurdle, child-rearing episode, and family tragedy.

This friend, with whom she had so often started their daily ride with sadness or crying and he had then magically transformed her mood to happy and laughing.

This friend, who had been a sounding board for every bad workday and major career decision.

This friend, who had carried her through her greatest triumphs and her saddest moments and who had made her a stronger and better person.

This friend, with whom she had bound her very soul and inner spirit.

This friend, who had had been as honest as the day is long.

This friend, who had unselfishly devoted his entire existence to her happiness, never hesitating to give his all whenever she asked it of him.

This friend, whose careful manners and loving attitude had given her immeasurable joy and unending sanctuary.

How could she let him go from her life, and yet how could she not? Tears streamed down her face as she gave him a long and final hug. The embrace cut through the bitter cold air and warmed her very soul, just as it had the very first time she had stepped the baby horse from the trailer and hugged his soft, tiny neck; promising to take care of him forever.

"*Forever*" had not lasted as long as it should have, and she was not yet ready to let go of the one friend who had seen her through every event of her life for nearly thirty years.

Something deep inside her hurt like it had never hurt before . . . and she felt very alone and sad.

She knew that she had no choice, and so she placed a long and final goodbye kiss on his moist eyelashes. It was then she realized that he too was crying.

The woman, who suddenly felt very old and very alone, lovingly whispered the sad final words in his limp ear, "*Goodbye old friend, I will miss you . . . always . . .*"

About the Author

I was born in the United States in a small rural county in the tip of the thumb of Michigan. This peninsula is surrounded on three sides by beautiful Lake Huron, one of the five freshwater lakes of the Great Lakes. It was a wondrous, bountiful, and natural environment in which a child could explore and thrive for it was abundant with hundreds of miles of sandy shoreline, beautiful woods, clear babbling streams and rivers, and thousands of acres of some of the richest most fertile farmland anywhere in the United States.

During my childhood, nearly everyone in the community earned their livings from some type of farming or agricultural business (crops, dairy, beef, etc). My parents were somewhat of an exception at that time, because they both had college degrees. My father was a schoolteacher and my mother was a registered nurse. Additionally, they operated our family fruit orchard.

Growing up in this remote rural environment in a family of six children, life was always bustling with activity which focused on maintaining and assuring for the needs of the family. The family sustained itself by growing huge summer gardens, maintaining the fruit orchard, raising chickens for eggs, hunting, fishing, and trapping. We canned the goods from our harvest throughout the summer and stored bushels of produce for the long cold Michigan winters. It prepared me and my siblings to be self-sufficient and to care for the land that provided for our needs.

I have endeavored to raise my own two sons with the same work ethic, values, and morals and to instill in them a love for nature and animals. My strong passion for animals and, in particular for horses and ponies, has given me unending joy and a nucleus for the family's connectedness.

As I am aging, I notice on an ever increasing basis, that I enjoy the simpler pleasures in life and have less attraction to the expectations of society. My life on the farm is perfect for me because animals are so undemanding and unpretentious. They are exactly what their behaviors and personalities say they are... nothing more and nothing less.

When I'm not at work or working on the farm with my horses and ponies, I enjoy quilting, writing, working with fibers, gardening and creating hand-made heirlooms for future generations.

www.ingramcontent.com/pod-product-compliance
Lightning Source LLC
Chambersburg PA
CBHW021241280526
45784CB00005B/2183

* 9 7 8 1 4 3 8 9 4 7 9 0 7 *